String Art

By Rini Jose

Contents

Acknowledgement

There are a lot of people to Thank who helped me to make this happen. It was a very difficult task for a person like me to accomplish this task: Writing and publishing a book. Thanks to all who supported and encouraged me to achieve the same. Very much thanks to everyone for all the help and support.

Introduction

String art is one of the art which doesn't require any special skills. But it is an art which need patience. Most of the artist is making string art by using string and nails. String art is one of the most satisfying art in the world. The main attractiveness of this art is as I have already mentioned, you don't need any high level training or knowledge to start doing the same which makes it very easy. The result is very satisfying even if it is a simple task to complete a string art design. Anyone at any age (not for very young kids) can start doing string art.

String art designs can be geometric designs or patterns like: String Art Circle Pattern, String Art triangle pattern, String Art Rectangle Pattern, String Art Square Pattern, String Art Star Pattern, String Art Pentagon pattern, String Art Hexagon Pattern, String Art Octagon Pattern. String art designs can be letters like names or individual letter art. String art designs can be some objects like heart (love), star, anchor, etc.

I have created this book for beginners who like to create beautiful string art. This book has all the tips and tricks to start string art as a profession.

Tools and Materials

There are lot of tools which can be used to make string art. But I have mentioned the most basic tools and materials so that anyone can start their own string art without any delay. I will be explaining about the tools later in this book while explaining the step by step process.

1. Wooden board : 2 X 2 feet (24 X 24 inches)
2. Pencil, Ruler, Protractor
3. Design diagram
4. Tape
5. Scissors (small)
6. Nails (0.75 inch)
7. Hammer (small)
8. String 1 mm thickness (11 rainbow colors: Violet, Indigo, Blue, etc.; or you can use single color for the whole design)

Create Platform ready for String art

Wooden Board

Dimensions:

Width: 2 feet (24 inches)

Length: 2 feet (24 inches)

Thickness: 1 inch

Wooden Board Color:

Wooden board can be any color but the color should be opposite of the color of string, if the string is light-color then the wooden board should be dark-color or vice versa. It may not be possible to see the string art if the background is as same as the string color. You can use paint to color the background or you can wrap the wooden board by using leather sheets, fabrics, color paper, etc.

Wooden Board Type:

Wooden board should be lightweight but it should not crack while hammering the nails. It also should be hard wood because the nails should not come out while tightening the string.

Design Diagram

Draw the design diagram in a paper:

Don't draw the diagram directly on the wooden board because it will be very hard to remove/ erase the design once the nails are placed.

The paper size should be 2 X 2 feet (24 X 24 inches). It doesn't have to be one single paper, you can combine/ Tape four A4 papers to get the size.

Marking points:

Draw a circle with radius 11 inches.
Divide the circle by 2 degrees using a protractor.
Mark points on the design diagram for placing the nails.

Tape the Design Diagram on the wooden board

Tape the design diagram on the wooden board so that it won't move while hammering the nails.

Hammer the nails

Hammer the nails into the marked points

Insert 30 to 40% of a nail into the wooden board otherwise it may come out while tightening the string.

Remove paper diagram

Remove the paper diagram from the wooden board once you have placed the nails. You will get a platform as shown below once you have completed all the mentioned steps.

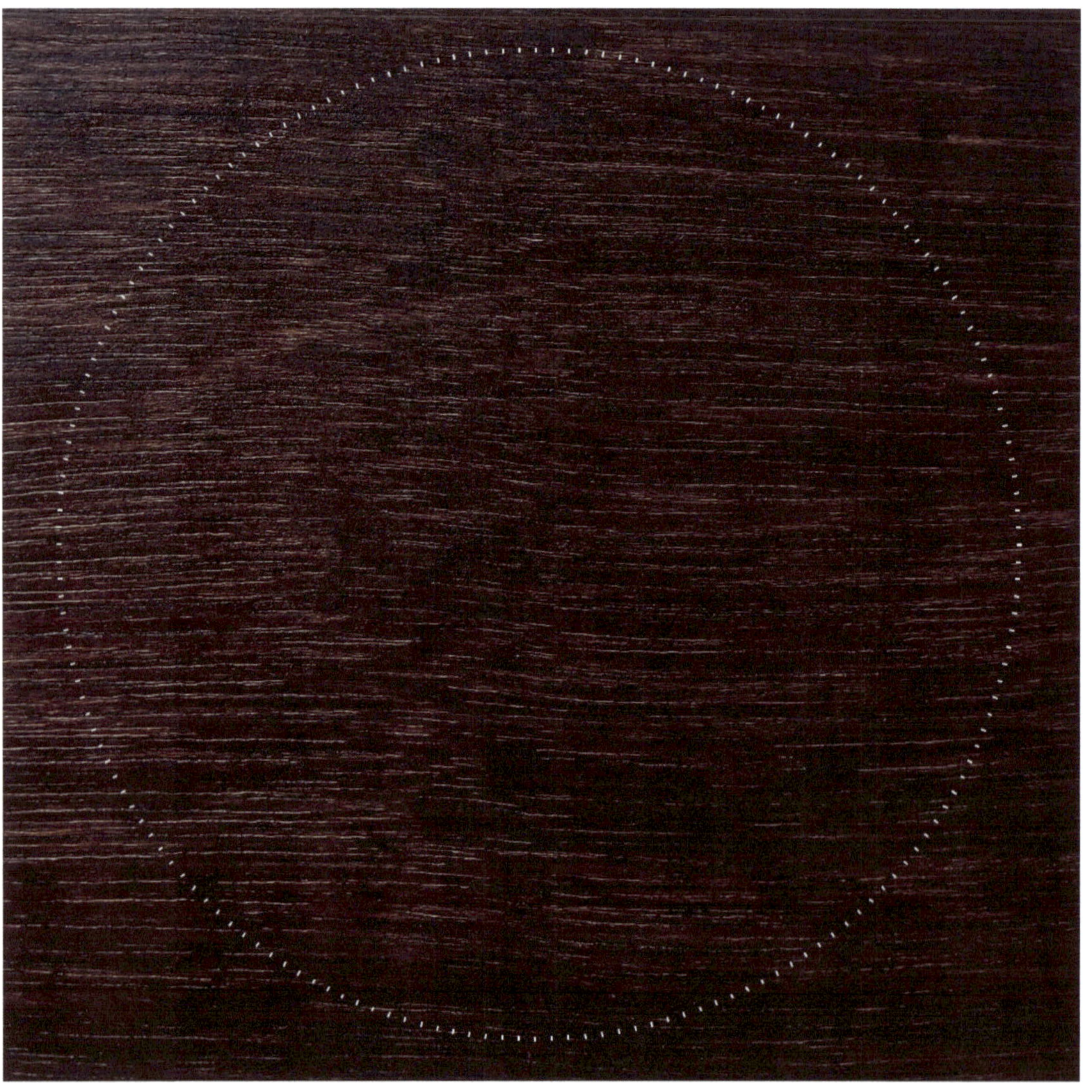

Step by step process to make string art

You will get the final piece of art as shown below once you have completed the following steps.

Cycle-1

Select any nail point and tie the string onto that nail. I'm mentioning the selected nail as '1'. I have used the white string for showing the basic steps but you can use your own color for the same.

Note: For this design pattern. You need to connect the string from one point to the double of that point. (For example: if the point is Nail-4 then, you need to connect the string from nail-4 to nail-8).

Note: Always wrap the string around the nail when you connect the string from one nail to another one. You don't need to tie the string on every nails but just wrap around the nail.

1. Start
2. Connect the string from nail-1 to nail-2.

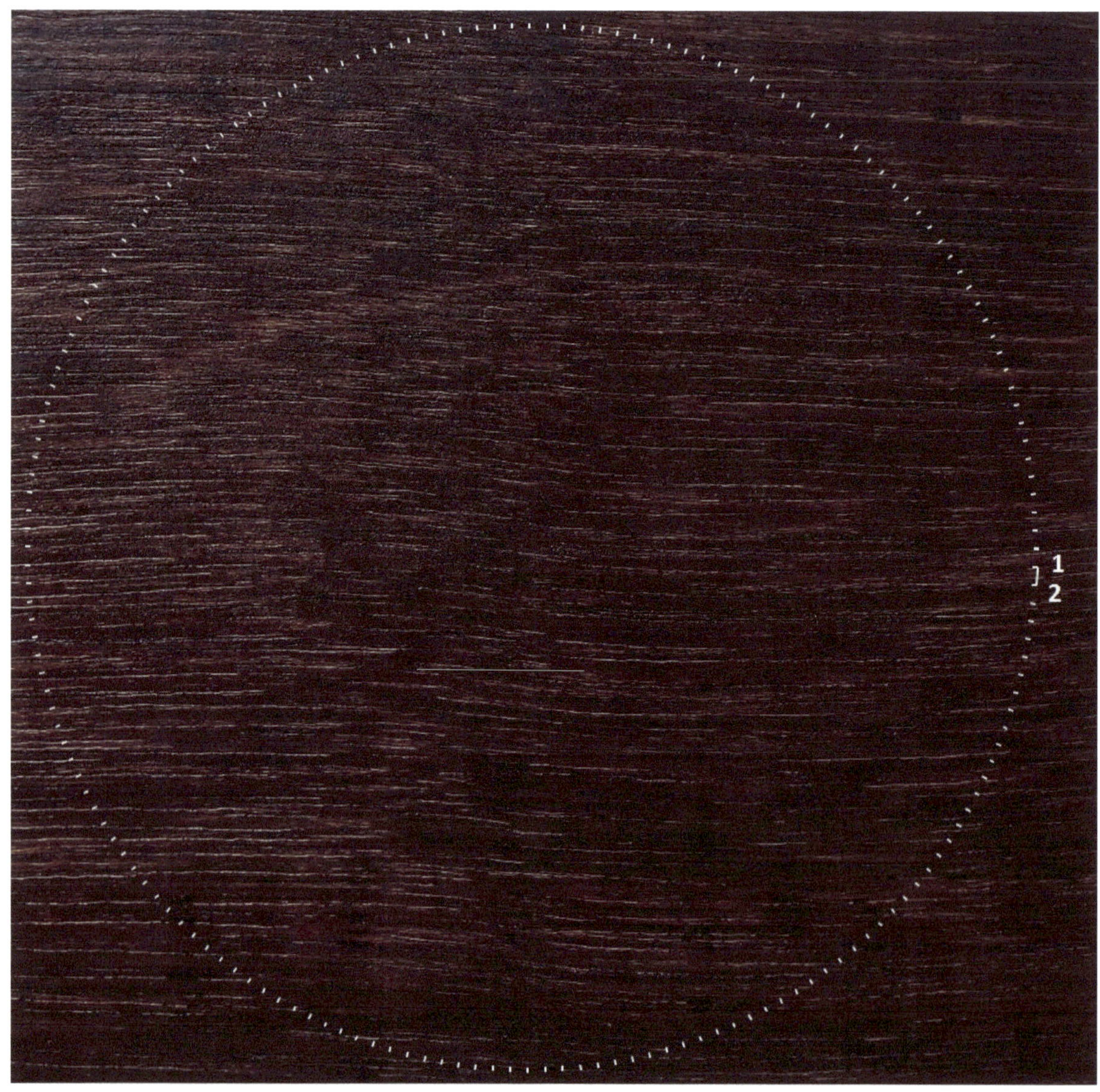

3. Connect the string from nail-2 to nail-4. Then, connect the string back to Nail-3.

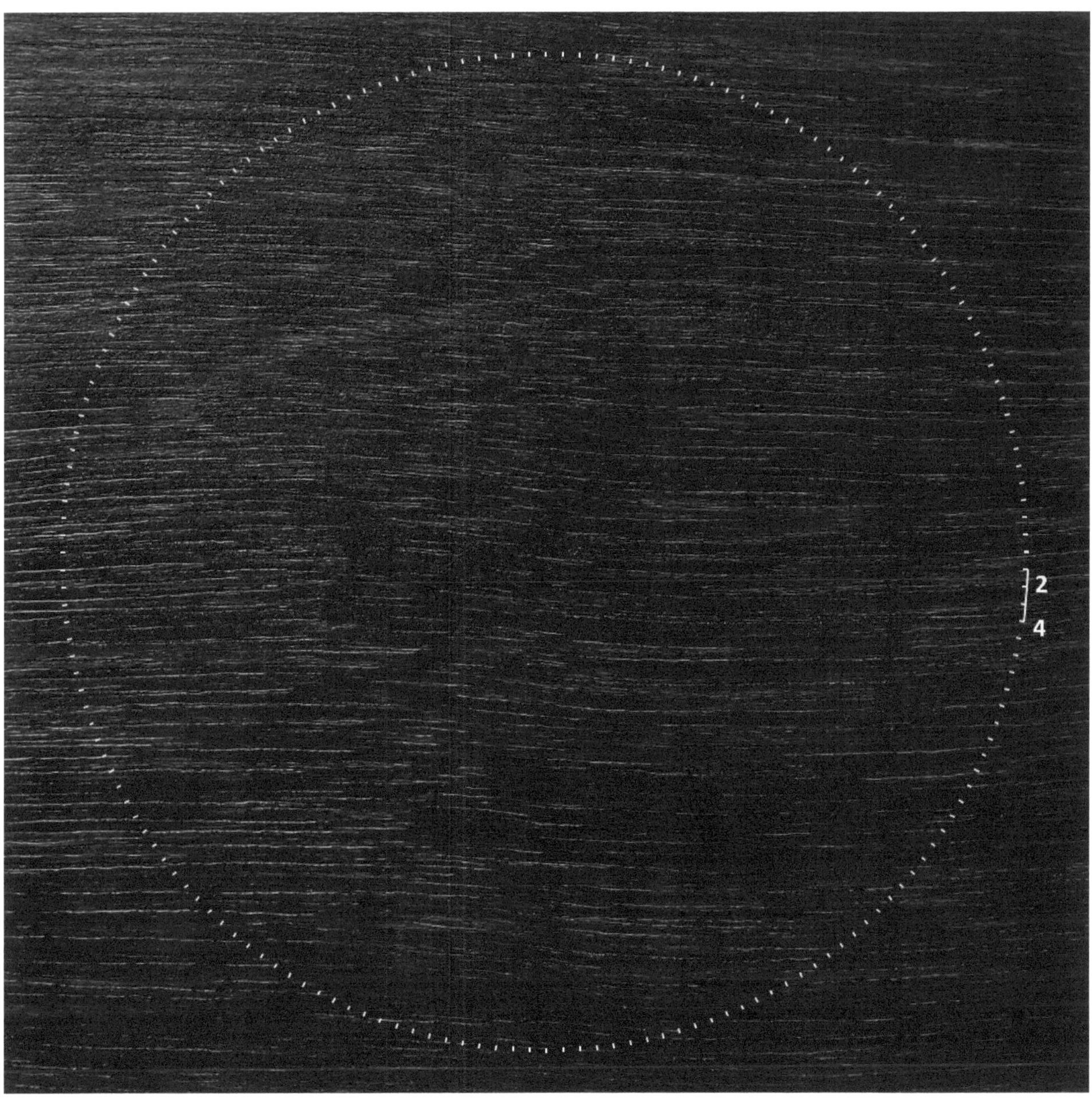

4. Connect the string from nail-3 to nail-6. Then connect the string back to Nail-4.

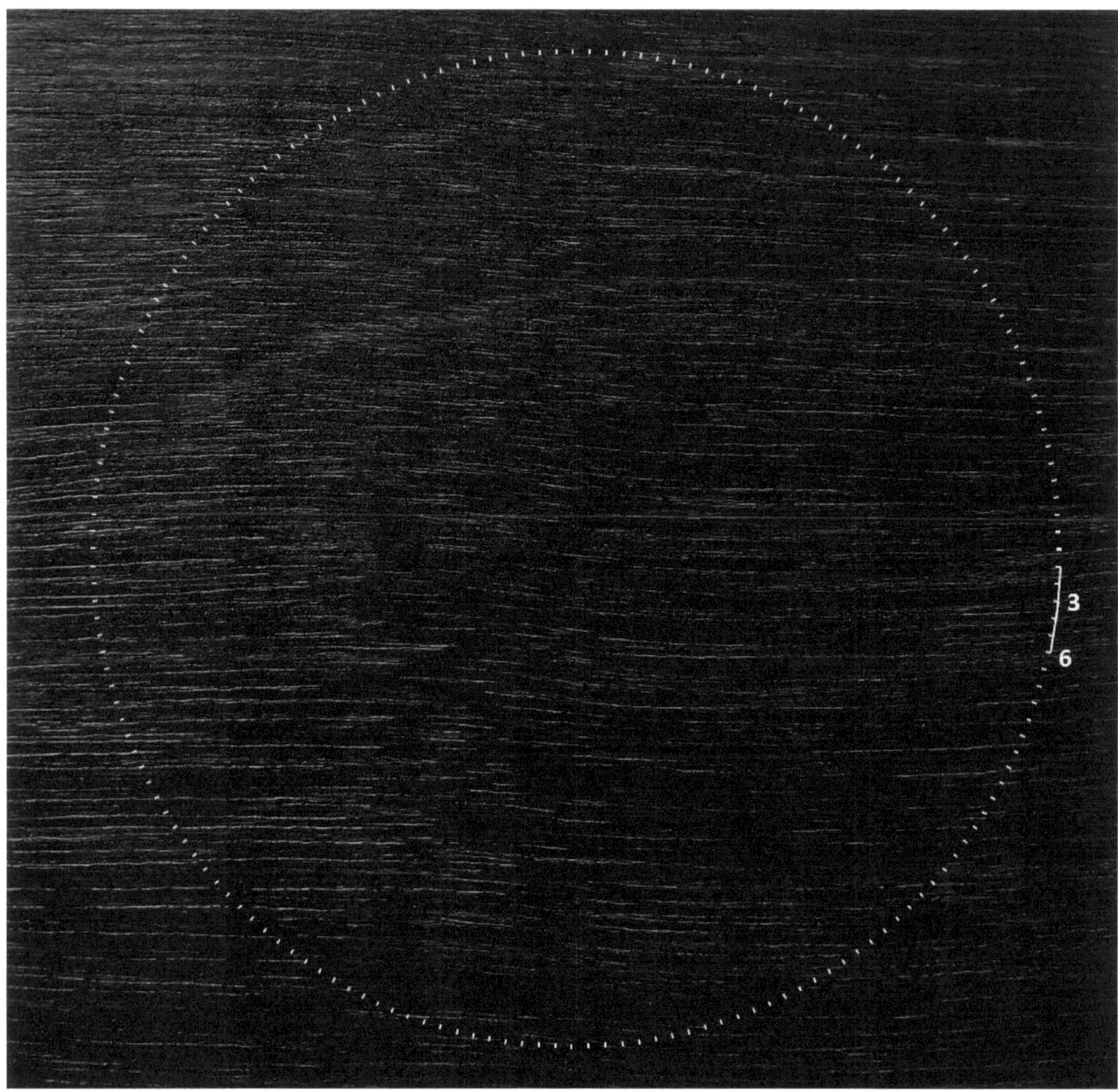

5. Connect the string from nail-4 to nail-8. Then connect the string back to Nail-5.

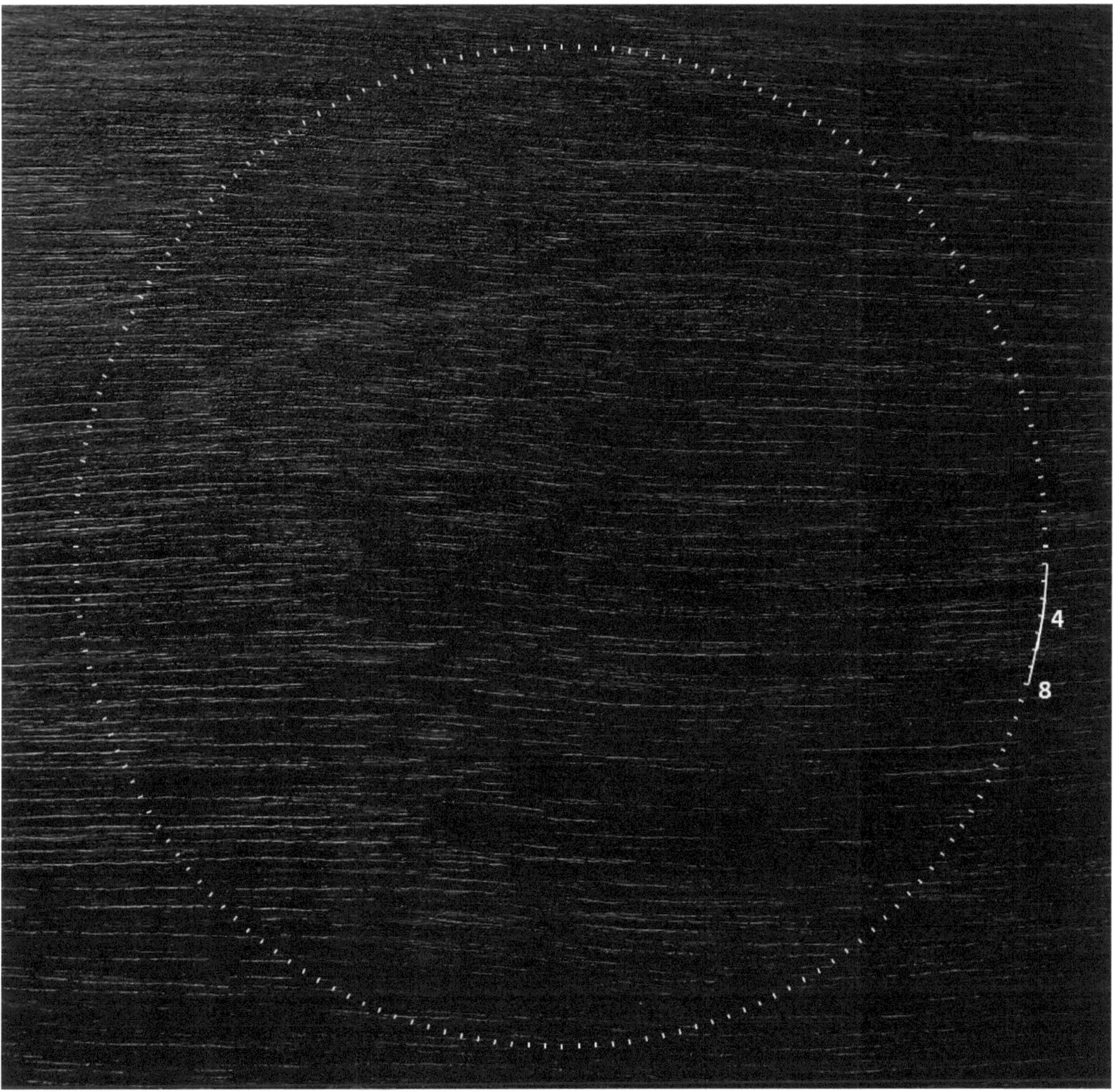

6. Connect the string from nail-5 to nail-10. Then connect the string back to Nail-6.

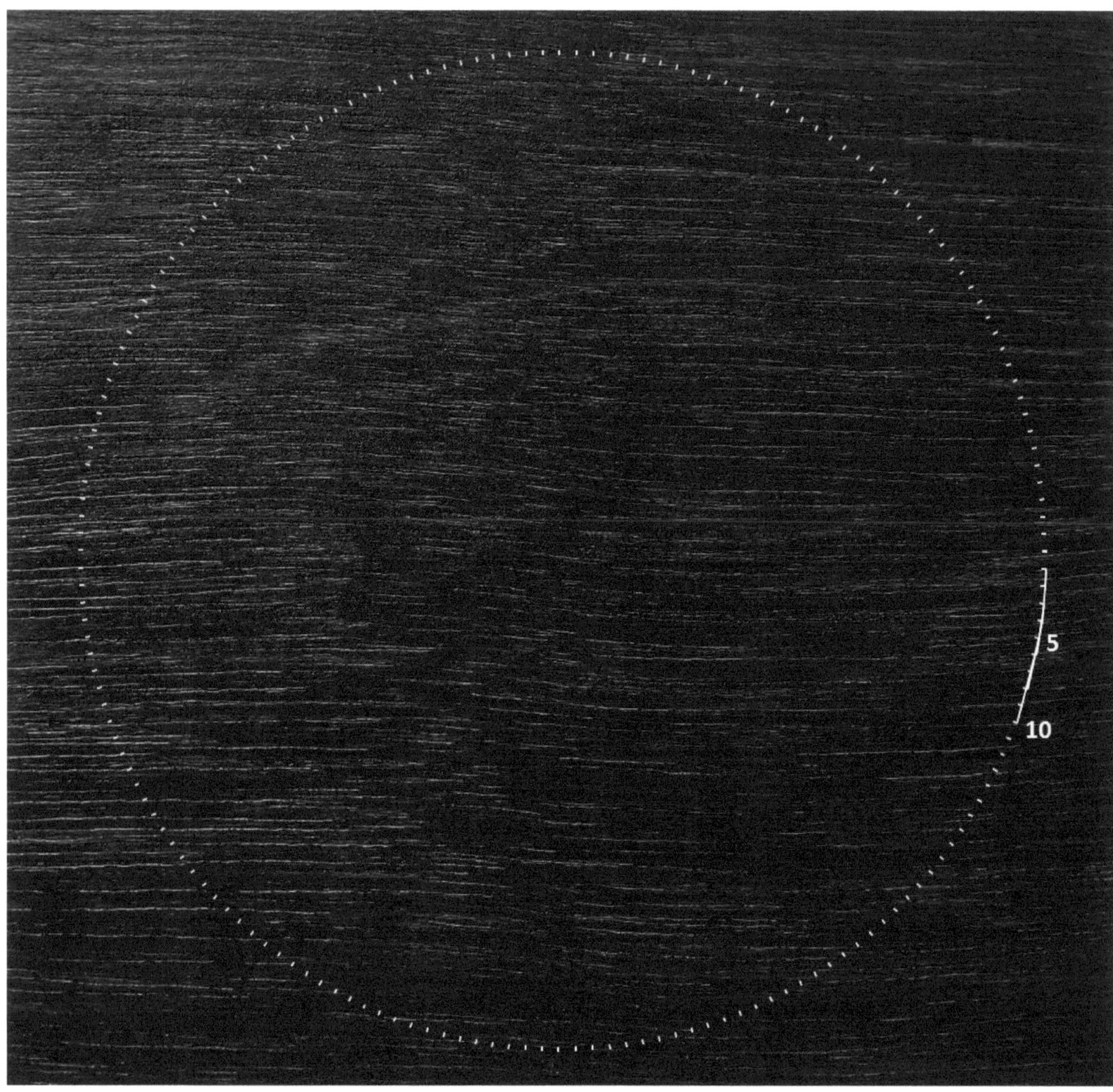

7. Connect the string from nail-6 to nail-12. Then connect the string back to Nail-7.

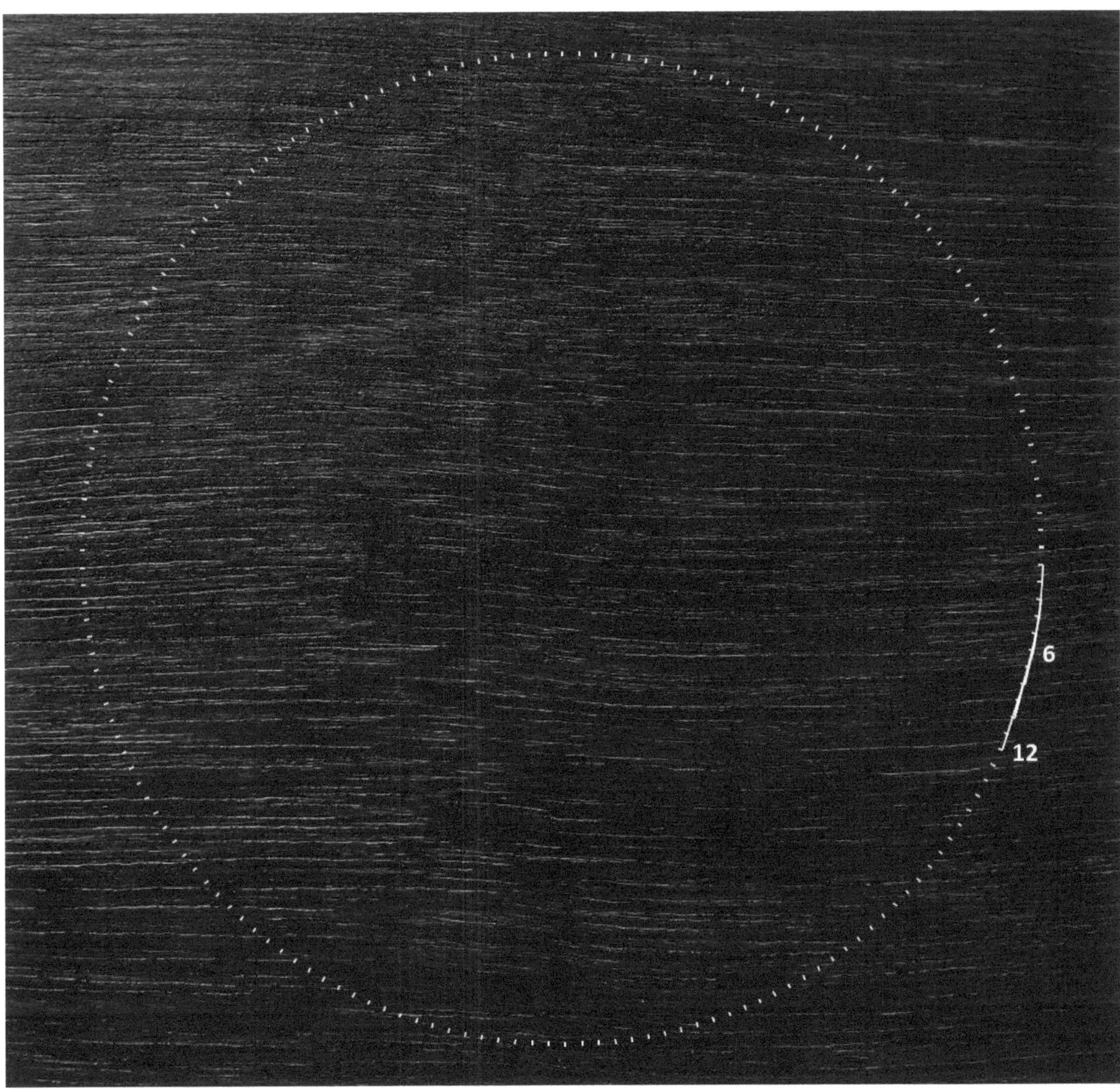

8. Connect the string from nail-7 to nail-14. Then connect the string back to Nail-8.

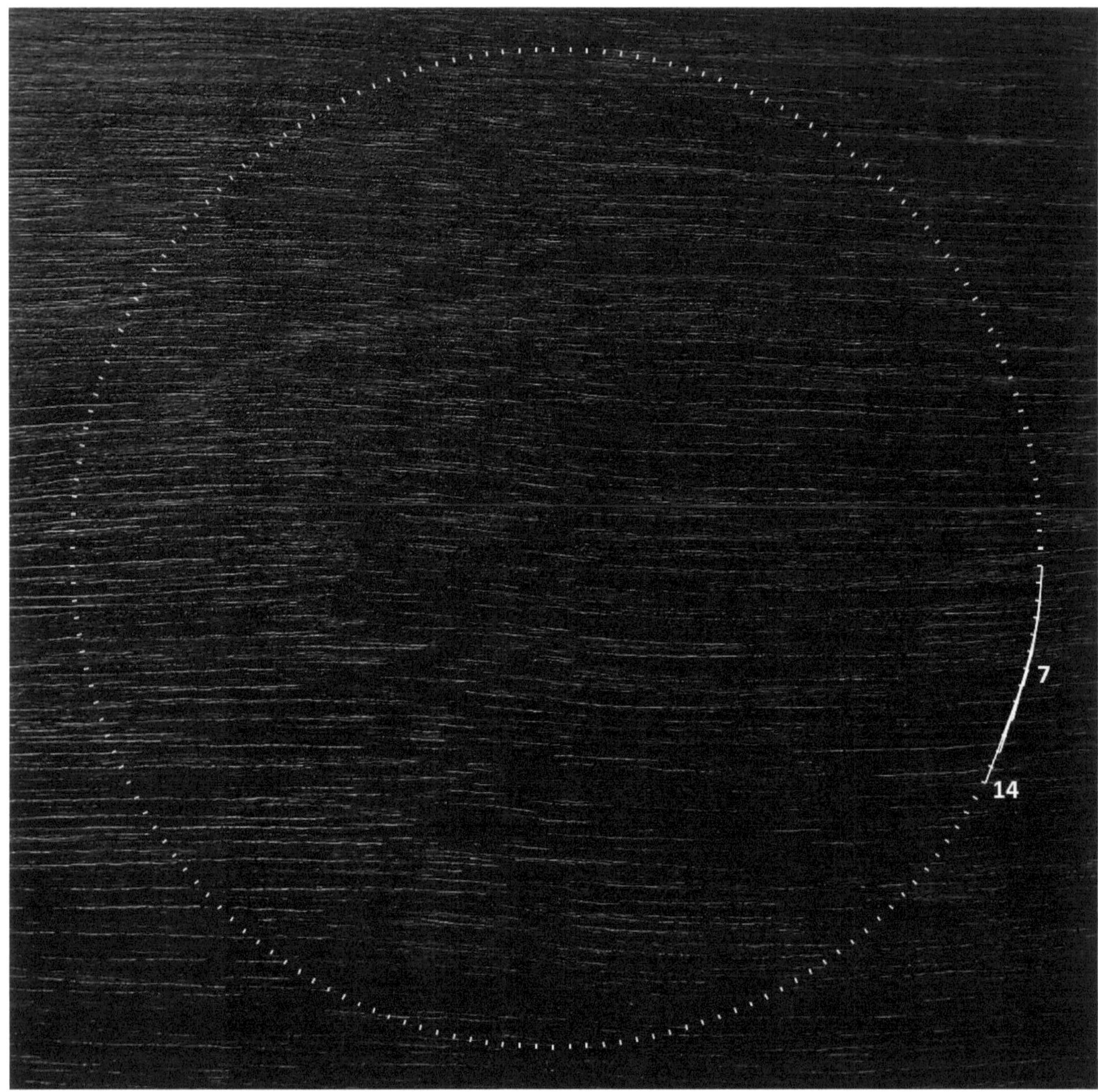

9. Continue the process.

Continue this process until you reach the starting point. Tie the string onto that nail once the string reached the starting point. You will get the result as shown below:

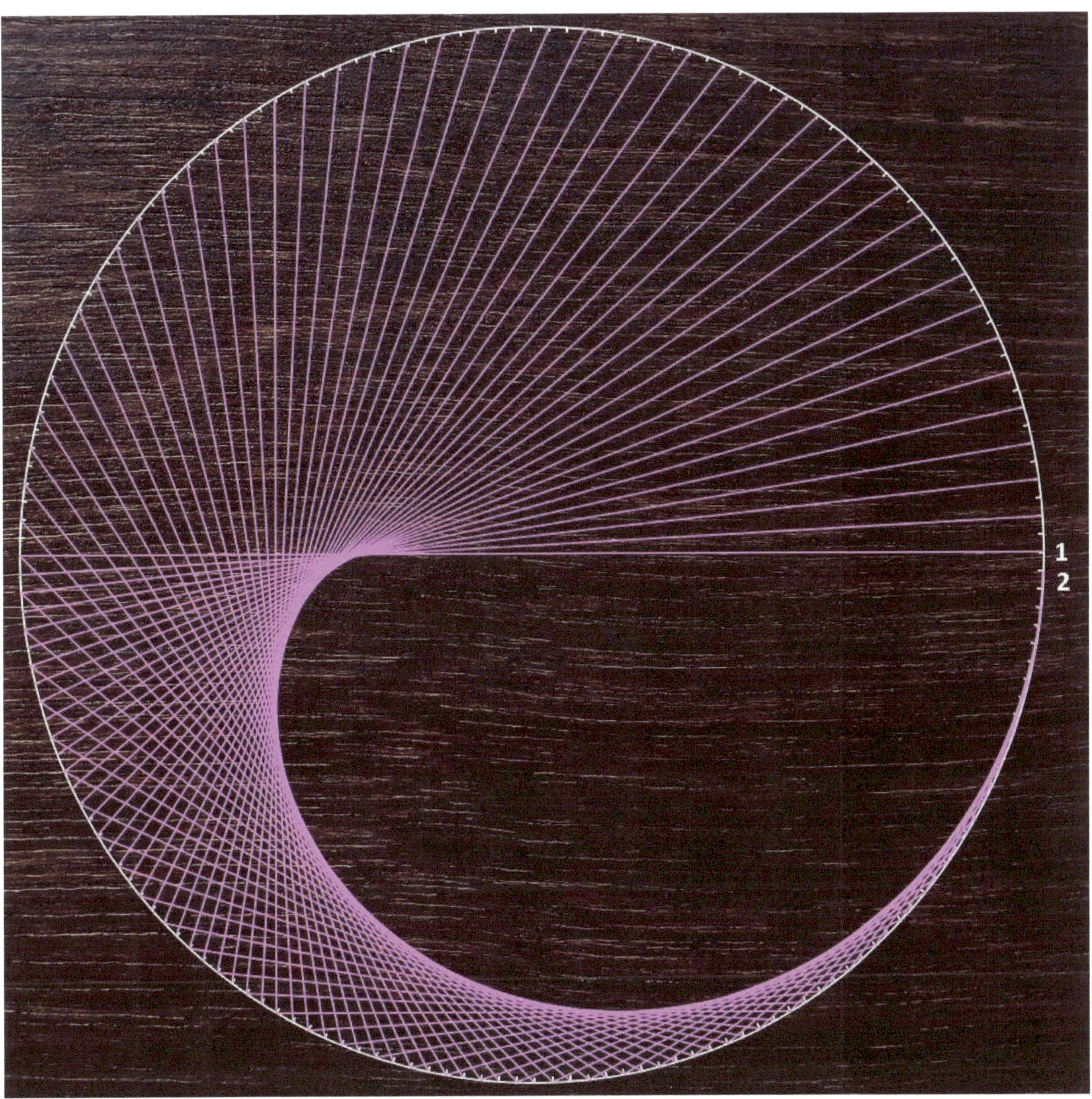

Cycle-2

Select 16th nail point from the first nail point and tie the string onto that nail. And then, select that nail as '1' so that it would be easy for you to repeat the previous process and complete cycle-2. The gap between the 2 cycles should be almost equal to get a beautiful string art.

Repeat the same process and you will get the result as shown below:

Cycle-3

Select 33rd nail point from the first nail point (first nail point in Cycle-1) and tie the string onto that nail. And then, select that nail as '1' so that it would be easy for you to repeat the previous process and complete cycle-3. As I have mentioned before, the gap between the 2 cycles should be almost equal to get a beautiful string art.

Repeat the same process and you will get the result as shown below:

Cycle-4

Select 50th nail point from the first nail point (first nail point in Cycle-1) and tie the string onto that nail. And then, select that nail as '1' so that it would be easy for you to repeat the previous process and complete cycle-4.

Note: *All the cycle process is same. The only change is the starting point.*

Repeat the same process and you will get the result as shown below:

Cycle-5

Select 67th nail point from the first nail point (first nail point in Cycle-1) and tie the string onto that nail. And then, select that nail as '1' so that it would be easy for you to repeat the previous process and complete cycle-5.

Note: *All the cycle process is same. The only change is the starting point.*

Repeat the same process and you will get the result as shown below:

Cycle-6

Select 84th nail point from the first nail point (first nail point in Cycle-1) and tie the string onto that nail. And then, select that nail as '1' so that it would be easy for you to repeat the previous process and complete cycle-6.

Note: All the cycle process is same. The only change is the starting point.

Repeat the same process and you will get the result as shown below:

Cycle-7

Select 100th nail point from the first nail point (first nail point in Cycle-1) and tie the string onto that nail. And then, select that nail as '1' so that it would be easy for you to repeat the previous process and complete cycle-7.

Note: All the cycle process is same. The only change is the starting point.

Repeat the same process and you will get the result as shown below:

Cycle-8

Select 116th nail point from the first nail point (first nail point in Cycle-1) and tie the string onto that nail. And then, select that nail as '1' so that it would be easy for you to repeat the previous process and complete cycle-8.

Note: *All the cycle process is same. The only change is the starting point.*

Repeat the same process and you will get the result as shown below:

Cycle-9

Select 132nd nail point from the first nail point (first nail point in Cycle-1) and tie the string onto that nail. And then, select that nail as '1' so that it would be easy for you to repeat the previous process and complete cycle-9.

Note: *All the cycle process is same. The only change is the starting point.*

Repeat the same process and you will get the result as shown below:

Cycle-10

Select 148th nail point from the first nail point (first nail point in Cycle-1) and tie the string onto that nail. And then, select that nail as '1' so that it would be easy for you to repeat the previous process and complete cycle-10.

Note: All the cycle process is same. The only change is the starting point.

Repeat the same process and you will get the result as shown below:

Cycle-11

Select 165th nail point from the first nail point (first nail point in Cycle-1) and tie the string onto that nail. And then, select that nail as '1' so that it would be easy for you to repeat the previous process and complete cycle-11.

Note: *All the cycle process is same. The only change is the starting point.*

Repeat the same process and you will get the result as shown below:

Final Result

All Cycles

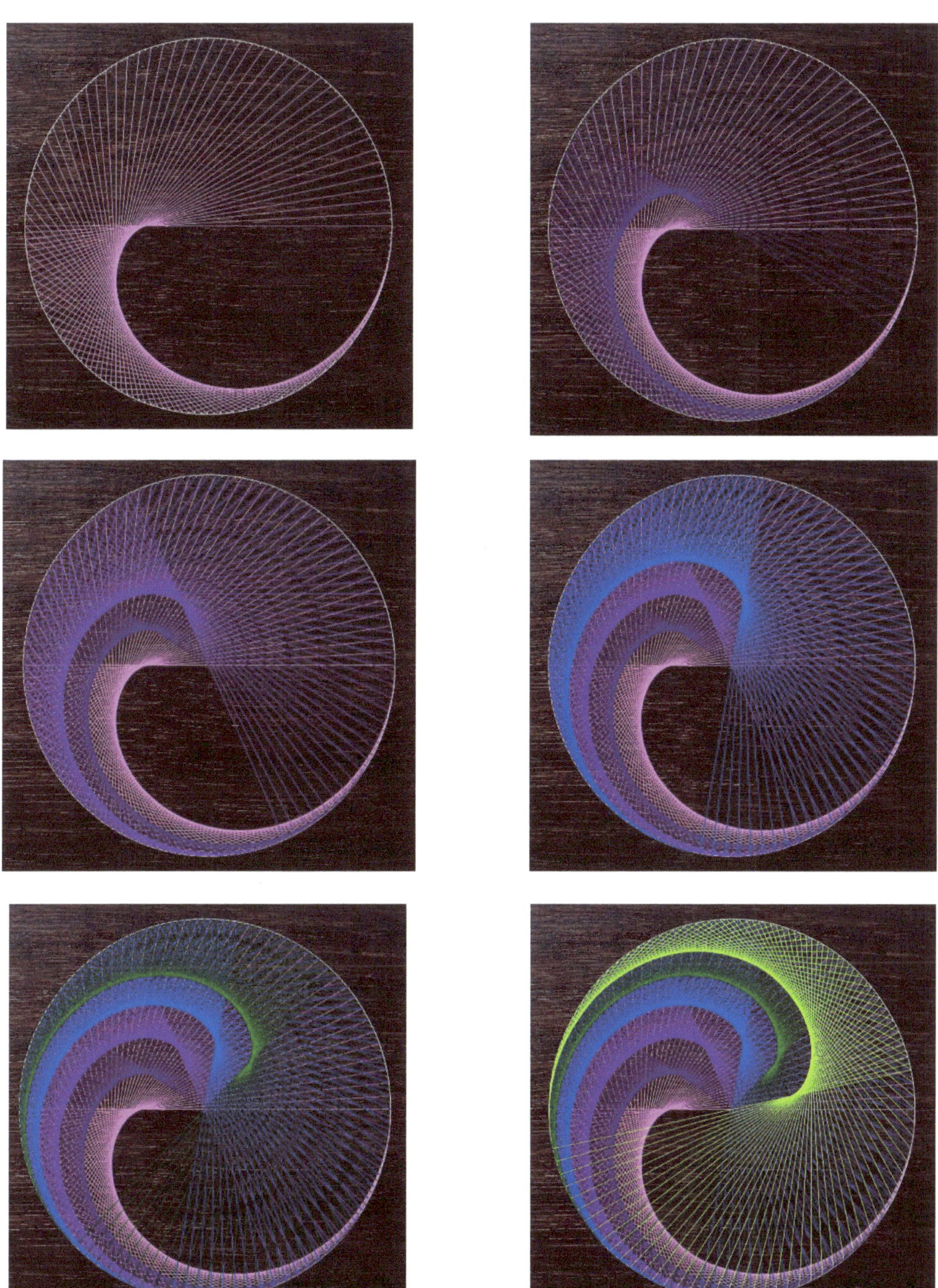

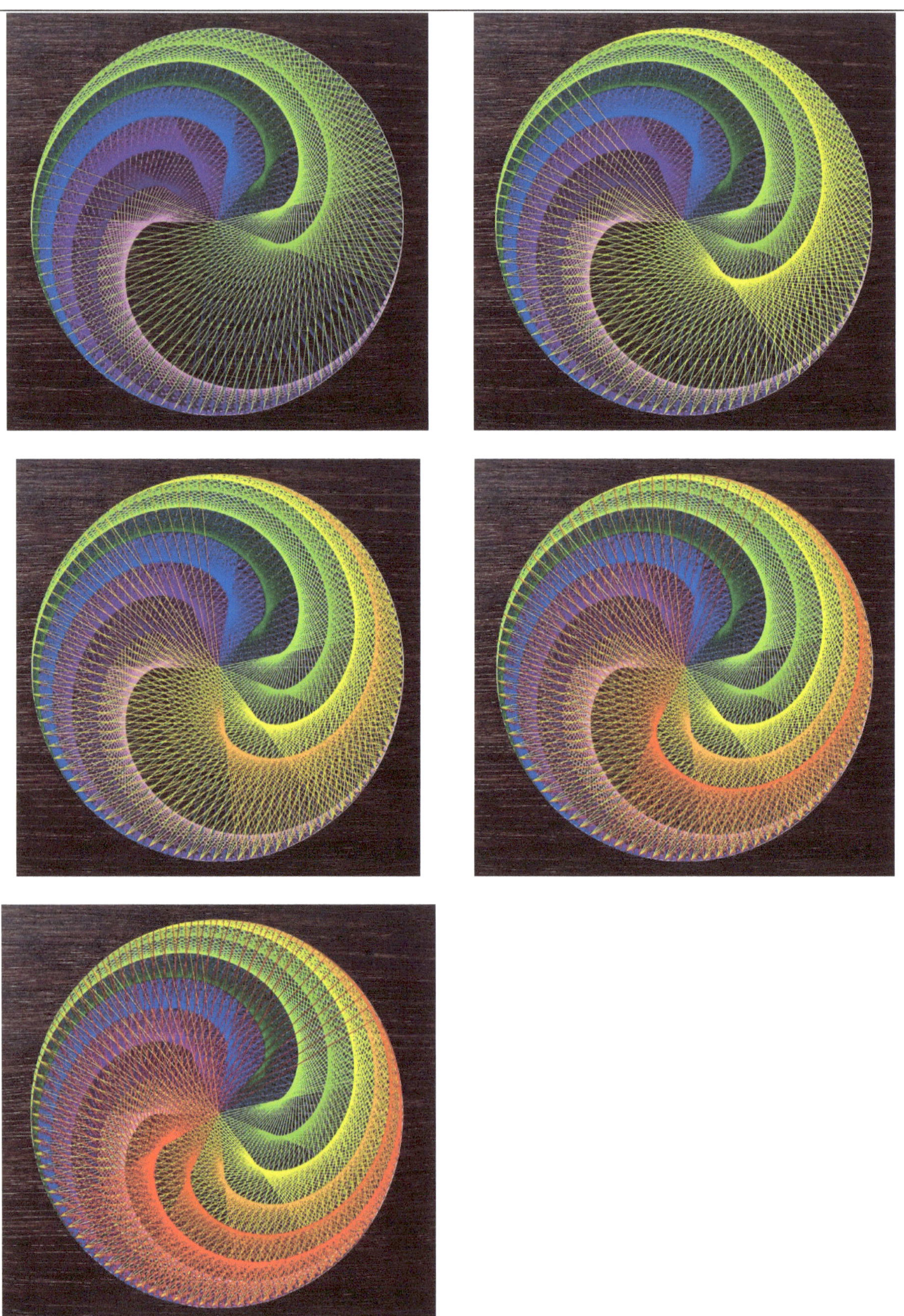

Coming soon